D1146096

The Silly Little Book

of

COOL JOKES

The Silly Little Book of

COOL JOKES

This is a Parragon Book first published 2000

Parragon
Queen Street House
4 Queen Street
Bath BA1 1HE

Produced by Magpie Books, an imprint of
Robinson Publishing Ltd, London

ISBN 0 75253 480 7

A copy of the British Library Cataloguing-in-Publication Data
is available from the British Library

Printed and bound in Singapore

Contents

Ice Breakers

Why did the cat put the letter "M" into the fridge?
Because it turns ice into mice.

Why is a polar bear cheap to have as a pet?
It lives on ice.

What was the fly doing on the ice cream?
Learning to ski.

What kind of money do yetis use?
Iced lolly.

What does a Yeti eat for dinner?
Iceburgers.

How do ghosts like their drinks?
Ice ghoul.

What do you get if you cross a
witch with an iceberg?
A cold spell.

Two witches lost their brooms and
crash-landed on an iceberg.
"Do you think we'll be here long?"
asked the first. "No," said the
second, "here comes the Titanic."

Waiter, waiter! What's this cockroach doing on my ice-cream sundae?
I think it's skiing downhill.

What happened when the ice monster had a furious row with the zombie?
He gave him the cold shoulder.

What's the difference between an
iced lolly and the school bully?
You lick one, the others lick you.

What happened when the Ice
Monster ate a curry?
He blew his cool.

Simon: My girlfriend and I fell out last night. She wanted to go and watch ice-skating, but I wanted to go to the football match.
Peter: What was the ice-skating like?

What takes a lot of licks from a teacher without complaint?
An ice cream.

On their first evening in their new home the bride went into the kitchen to fix the drinks.

Five minutes she came back into the living-room in tears.

"What's the matter, my angel?" asked her husband anxiously.

"Oh Derek!" she sobbed, "I put the ice-cubes in hot water to wash them and they've disappeared!"

A family of tortoises went into a café for some ice cream. They sat down and were about to start when Father Tortoise said, "I think its gong to rain, Junior, will you pop home and fetch my umbrella?" So off went Junior for Father's umbrella, but three days later he still hadn't returned. "I think, dear," said Mother Tortoise to Father Tortoise, "that we had better eat Junior's ice cream before it melts." And a voice from the door said, "If you do that I won't go."

One very hot day an extremely small man went into a café, put his newspaper on a table and went to the counter. But on returning with a cup of tea he saw that his place had been taken by a huge, bearded, ferocious-looking man of some 300 pounds in weight, and six feet nine inches in height. "Excuse me," said the little man to the big man, "but you're sitting in my seat." "Oh yeah?" snarled the big man. "Prove it!" "Certainly. You're sitting on my ice cream."

What did the Eskimo schoolboy
say to the Eskimo schoolgirl?
What's an ice girl like you doing in
a place like this?

What did Tom get when he locked
Jerry in the freezer?
Mice cubes.

Notice by a village pond: Beware!
All of this ice is frozen.

Wally: If frozen water is iced water,
what is frozen ink?
Sally: Iced ink.

Teacher: Order, children, order!
Daft Derek: Two chocolate ice creams and three orange lollipops, please.

Why did Darren put his father in the freezer?
He wanted ice-cold pop.

How do you know if an elephant's been in your fridge?
There are footprints in the butter.

Why did the stupid witch keep her
clothes in the fridge?
She liked to have something cool
to slip into in the evening.

A woman went to the fridge to get
some milk and all she found was
a disembodied hand there.
It was all fingers and thumbs.

Why did Ken keep his trumpet in
the fridge?
Because he liked cool music.

Cannibal Boy: I've brought a friend
home for dinner.
Cannibal Mom: Put him in the
fridge and we'll have him
tomorrow.

What do you call the famous Italian artist who did his paintings sitting on the fridge?
Bottichilli.

Did you hear about the mad scientist who put dynamite in his fridge?
They say he blew his cool.

What stays hot in the fridge?
A hamburger with too much
mustard on it.

What did the mayonnaise say to
the fridge?
"Shut the door, I'm dressing."

What is brown one minute and
white the next?
A rat in a deep-freeze.

Angela had to write down on her exam paper the name of a liquid that won't freeze, so she wrote "hot water."

What did the Eskimo children sing when one of their class was leaving school?
"Freeze a jolly good fellow."

Why did the monster drink ten
liters of anti-freeze?
So that he didn't have to buy a
winter coat.

Why did the snowman call his dog
Frost?
Because frost bites.

What's another way to describe a
duck?
A chicken with snowshoes.

Teacher: Who knows what we mean by the Cold War?
Larry: Err, a snowball fight?

What exams do Yetis take?
Snow levels.

Can the Abominable Snowman
jump very high?
Hardly – he can only just clear his
throat!

What kind of man doesn't like to
sit in front of the fire?
An Abominable Snowman.

How do Abominable Snowmen feel
when they melt?
Abominable!

What do Abominable Snowmen
call their offspring?
Chill-dren.

Where do Abominable Snowmen
go to dance?
To snowballs.

What did one Abominable
Snowman say to the other?
I'm afraid I just don't believe in
people.

What is the Abominable
Snowman's favorite book?
War and Frozen Peas.

What did the Abominable
Snowman do after he had had his
teeth pulled out?
He ate the dentist.

Why did the skeleton stay out in
the snow all night?
He was a numbskull.

I Met An Abominable Snowman –
by Anne Tarctic.

There was a young yeti from
Gloucester
Whose granny and grandfather
lost 'er.
Next day she was found
In the snow-covered ground
But they didn't know how to
defrost her.

Doctor, doctor! I keep thinking I'm
the Abominable Snowman.
Keep cool.

What does it mean if you have an elephant in your fridge?
He slept over, after the great party you had last night.

Did you hear about the woman who was so keen on road safety that she always wore white at night?
Last winter she was knocked down by a snow plow.

Billy: I never had a sledge when I was a kid. We were too poor.
Milly, feeling sorry for him: What a shame! What did you do when it snowed?
Billy: Slid down the hills on my cousin.

Why was the snowman no good at playing in the big match?
He got cold feet.

Ted and Fred were enjoying themselves in the snow. "You can borrow my sledge if you like," said Ted. "Thanks," said Fred. "We'll share it, shall we?" "Yes," said Ted. "I'll have it going downhill and you can have it going uphill."

Cooler Cracks

Two shark fishermen were sitting on the side of their boat just off the coast of Florida, cooling their feet in the sea. Suddenly an enormous shark swam up and bit off one fisherman's leg. "A shark's just bitten off my leg," yelled the fisherman. "Which one?"

What kind of cats love water?
Octopuses.

Bertie: My mom asked the doctor
for something for wind.
Gertie: What did he do?
Bertie: He gave her a kite.

Kevin: I'm really cool, you know.
Kieran: I always thought you were
a cold fish.

Why is a football stadium cool?
It's full of fans.

How do you know if your cat's got
a bad cold?
He has cat-arrh.

What do you give a pony with a
cold?
Cough Stirrup.

What does an octopus wear when
it's cold?
A coat of arms.

What goes "hum-choo, hum-choo"
A bee with a cold.

What's a cold, evil candle called?
The wicked wick of the north.

What kind of medicine does
Dracula take for a cold?
Coffin medicine.

What happened to the zombie who had a bad cold?
He said, "I'm dead-up wid fuddy jokes aboud zondies."

Werewolf: Doctor, doctor, thank you so much for curing me.
Doctor: So you don't think you're a werewolf anymore?
Werewolf: Absolutely not, I'm quite clear now – see my nose is nice and cold.

Doctor, doctor! What would you
take for this cold?
Make me an offer.

Why do skeletons hate winter?
Because the cold goes right
through them.

Doctor, doctor! How can I stop my
cold going to my chest?
Tie a knot in your neck.

Doctor, doctor! I keep thinking I'm a
dog out in the cold.
Oh, stop whining.

What happened when the ice
monster had a furious row with the
zombie?
He gave him the cold shoulder.

And what goes into the water pink
and comes out blue?
A swimmer on a cold day!

What's hairy and damp and sits
shivering at fairs?
A coconut with a cold.

What's the difference between a
bus driver and a cold?
One knows the stops; the other
stops the nose.

Why can you run faster when
you've got a cold?
Because you have a racing pulse
and a running nose.

George knocked on the door of his
friend's house.
When his friend's mother
answered he said: "Can Albert
come out to play?" "No," said the
mother, "it's too cold." "Well, then,"
said George. "can his football
come out to play?"

Geography teacher: What is the
coldest place in the world?
Ann: Chile.

What can a schoolboy keep and
give away at the same time?
A cold.

Did you hear about the snake with
a bad cold?
No! Tell me about the snake with a
bad cold.
She had to viper nose.

What is hairy and coughs?
A coconut with a cold.

Teacher: Matthew, what is the
climate of New Zealand?
Matthew: Very cold, sir.
Teacher: Wrong.
Matthew: But sir! When they send
us meat, it always arrives frozen!

Lady (to a tramp who's asked for a meal): Do you like cold prunes and custard?
Tramp: I love it, lady.
Lady: Well, call back later, it is very hot right now.

Young Horace was being taught how to box, but so far hadn't landed a single blow on his opponent.
"Don't worry, lad," said his teacher, "keep swinging – the draft might give him a cold."

It was raining, and the goalie had let several goals through. As he came off the pitch he sniffed, and said, "I think I've caught a cold."

"I'm pleased to hear you can catch something," replied a fellow player.

It was a warm day and the baseball player kept missing his shots. After the match he sighed and said, "What couldn't I do with a long, cold drink?"

"Hit it?" inquired a fellow player."

Billy: Is your cold better?
Tilly: I've got a very bad head but I hope to shake it off soon.

He's so cold-blooded that if a mosquito bit him it would get pneumonia.

You're like a summer cold!
What do you mean?
It's impossible to get rid of you!

What animal with two humps can
be found at the North Pole?
A lost camel.

Neddy: I've got a cold in the head.
Teddy: It must be the first time
you've had anything in your head.

How do sheep keep warm in
winter?
Central bleating.

What likes to spend the summer in a fur coat and the winter in a swimsuit?
A moth.

First cat: Where do fleas go in winter?
Second cat: Search me!

Waiter, waiter! There's a wasp in my pudding.
So that's where they go to in the winter.

Why don't vultures fly south in the winter?
Because they can't afford the air fare.

Teacher: Why do birds fly south in winter?
Jim: Because it's too far to walk.

Why did the canoeist take a water pistol with him?
So he could shoot the rapids.

What's thick, black, floats on water and shouts "Knickers!"?
Crude oil.

What do you get if you cross a bottle of water with an electric eel?
A bit of a shock really!

What insect can fly underwater?
A bluebottle in a submarine

What happens if you upset a
cannibal?
You get into hot water.

What do you call a witch who likes
the beach but is scared of the
water?
A chicken sand-witch.

Why are vampire families so close?
Because blood is thicker than
water.

What do you call an alien starship
that drips water?
A crying saucer.

"Now don't forget boys," the science teacher droned on, "If it wasn't for water we would never learn to swim. And if we'd never learned to swim, just think how many people would have drowned!"

That boy is so dirty, the only time he washes his ears is when he eats watermelon.

Did you hear about the idiot who made his chickens drink boiling water?
He thought they would lay hard boiled eggs.

Teacher: Martin, put some more water in the fish tank.
Martin: But, Sir, they haven't drunk the water I gave them yesterday.

Mrs Twigg took her class on a nature ramble. They went past a large duck pond. "Be careful not to fall in, children," she said, "the water's very deep." "But it can't be, Miss," said Susie, "it only comes up to the middle of those ducks."

Why did the music student have a piano in the bathroom?
Because he was practicing Handel's Water Music.

Doctor, doctor! I think I've been bitten by a vampire.
Drink this glass of water.
Will it make me better?
No, but I'll be able to see your neck leaks.

Anne: Ugh! The water in my glass is cloudy.
Dan, trying to impress his new girlfriend: It's all right, it's just the glass that hasn't been washed.

Daddy, daddy, can I have another glass of water please?

But that's the tenth one I've given you tonight.

Yes, but the baby's bedroom is still on fire.

When is the water in the shower room musical?

When it's piping hot.

Why did the teacher wear a
lifejacket at night?
Because she liked sleeping on a
waterbed, and couldn't swim!

Which is the ghost's favorite
stretch of water?
Lake Eerie.

Did you hear about the stupid
water-polo player?
His horse drowned . . .

What is full of holes but can hold water?
A sponge.

A man in a swimming pool was on the very top diving board. He poised, lifted his arms, and was about to dive when the attendant came running up, shouting, "Don't dive – there's no water in that pool!" "That's all right," said the man. "I can't swim!"

The food at the club dinner was awful. The soup tasted like dishwater, the fish was off, the meat was overcooked, and the vegetables were obviously old. The last straw for one member was the custard, which was thick and lumpy. "This meal is disgusting!" he roared. "And what's more, I'm going to bring it up at the AGM next week!"

Policeman: Why are you driving with a bucket of water on the passenger seat?
Motorist: So I can dip my headlights.

Jane: Have you noticed that your mother smells a bit funny these days?
Wayne: No. Why?
Jane: Well your sister told me she was giving her a bottle of toilet water for her birthday.

Sign in a café: The management has personally passed all drinking water in this establishment.

He's so dumb that after he'd watched a gardening program on TV he started watering the light bulbs.

I hear he's a very careful person. Well, he likes to economize on soap and water.

What happened to the yacht that sank in shark-infested waters?
It came back with a skeleton crew.

Why didn't the idiot go water-skiing when he was on holiday?
He couldn't find a sloping lake.
Notice by a river: When this sign is under water the towpath is flooded.

Mrs Green: How's your new house?
Mrs Brown: The roof needs
mending. In last week's storm rain
was coming down the walls like
water.

If we want to keep our heads
above water we must keep our ears
to the ground.

Bob: They say he has a waterproof voice.
Ted: What do you mean?
Bob: It can't be drowned out.

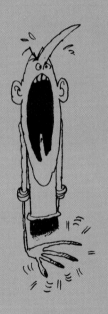

Ronnie: Why are you bathing in such dirty water?
Donnie: It wasn't dirty when I got in it.

How can I cure water on the knee?
Wear pumps.

Why do watermelons have to have a formal wedding?
Because they cant-elope.

Did you hear about the sailor that was discharged from the submarine service?
He was caught sleeping with the windows open.

Wasps – while everyone runs a mile when they see one, why does it take hours for them to work out how to get out of a room, even after you've opened the window that they're standing on?

Doctor: You need new glasses.
Monster: How did you guess?
Doctor: I could tell the moment you walked through the window.

Doctor, doctor! I keep thinking I'm a moth.
So why did you come to see me?
Well, I saw the light in the window…

A wizard went to the doctor one
day complaining of headaches.
"It's because I live in the same
room as two of my brothers," he
said. "One of them has six goats
and the other has four pigs and
they all live in the room with us.
The smell is terrible." "Well
couldn't you just open the
windows?" asked the doctor.
"Certainly not," he replied, "my
bats would fly out."

Art teacher: What color would you paint the sun and the wind?
Brian: The sun rose, and the wind blue.

How did the teacher forecast the weather with a piece of string?
She hung it up, and if it moved, she knew it was windy, and if it got wet, she knew it was raining.

Why does the Hound of the
Baskervilles turn round and round
before he lies down for the night?
Because he's the watchdog and
he has to wind himself up.

Doctor, doctor! I think I'm
Napoleon.
How long have you felt like this?
Since Waterloo.

Mr Jones met a neighbor carrying a front door. "Why are you carrying that, Tom?" asked Mr Jones.

"I've lost my key," replied Tom.

"Oh," said Mr Jones, "so how will you get in?"

"It's all right – I've left the window open."

Who broke the window?
It was Andrew, Dad. He ducked when I threw a stone at him.

A jeweler standing behind the counter of his shop was astounded to see a man come hurtling head first through the window. "What on earth are you up to?" he demanded. "I'm terribly sorry," said the man, "I forgot to let go of the brick!"

How do you cure a headache? Put your head through a window, and the pane will disappear.

Sign in shop window: FOR SALE
Pedigree bulldog. Housebroken.
Eats anything. Very fond of
children.

A man is in a prison cell with no
windows and no doors; there are
no holes in the ceiling or trapdoors
in the floor, yet in the morning the
wardens find him gone. How did
he get out?
Through the doorway – there were
no doors remember!

At a very posh wedding, one of the guests broke wind. The bridegroom was furious and rounded on the guilty party. "How dare you break wind in front of my wife?" he roared. "Sorry," said the guest. "Was it her turn?"

"Gosh, it's raining cats and dogs," said Suzie looking out of the kitchen window. "I know," said her mother who had just come in. "I've just stepped in a poodle!"

Dad, there's a man at the door collecting for the new swimming pool.
Give him a glass of water!

Who was the first underwater spy?
James Pond.

What happened when the bell fell in the water?
It got wringing wet.

Don't look out of the window, Lavinia, people will think it's Hallowe'en.

Dylan: I take lots of exercise.
Duncan: I thought so. That's why you're so long-winded.

What happened to the man who couldn't tell putty from custard? His windows fell out.

What happened to the man who couldn't tell the difference between putty and porridge? His teeth stuck together and his windows fell out.

Father: George! Don't let the dog hang his head out of the window whilst driving!

Red Hot Funnies

What do you get if you pour hot
water down a rabbit hole?
Hot cross bunnies!

It was so hot when we went on
holiday last year that we had to
take turns sitting in each other's
shadow.

What do you get if you cross a
snake with a hot dog?
A fangfurter.

What do frogs drink?
Hot croako.

What's white on the outside, green
on the inside and comes with
relish and onions?
A hot frog.

What happens if you eat a hot
frog?
You croak in no time.

What is the proper name for the
water otter?
A kettle.

What do witches ring for in a
hotel?
B-room service.

1st cannibal: I don't know what to
make of my husband.
2nd cannibal: How about a hotpot?

Hey, Waiter, you've got your thumb in my bowl of soup!
Don't worry, sir, the soup isn't hot.

It was sweltering hot outside. The teacher came into the classroom wiping his brow and said, "Ninety-two today. Ninety-two." "Happy birthday to you. Happy birthday to you . . ." sang the class.

When the class went on a trip to the seaside, they stayed at a small hotel that advertised Bed and Board. The trouble was, they said afterwards, it was difficult to know which was the bed and which was the board.

What did the teacher say after spending thousands in the expensive hotel?
"I'm sorry to leave, now that I've almost bought the place."

A man arrived at a seaside hotel where he had made a reservation rather late at night. All the lights were out, so he knocked on the door. After a long time a light appeared in an upstairs window and a woman called out, "Who are you? What do you want?" "I'm staying here." "Stay there, then," she retorted, and slammed the window shut!

Teacher: I'd like a room, please.
Hotel Receptionist: Single, Sir?
Teacher: Yes, but I am engaged.

There was a little old lady from a small town in America who had to go to Texas. She was amazed at the size of her hotel and her suite. She went into the huge cafe and said to the waitress, who took her order for a cup of coffee, that she had never before seen anything as big as the hotel or her suite. "Everything's big in Texas, ma'am," said the waitress. The coffee came in the biggest cup the old lady had ever seen. "I told you, ma'am that everything is big in Texas," said the waitress. On her way back to her suite, the old lady got lost in the vast corridors. She opened the door of a darkened room and fell into an enormous swimming pool. "Please!" she screamed. "Don't flush it!"

When we got to Benidorm the hotel was so full I had to sleep on a door across two tables. Was it comfortable?
Oh yes, but a bit drafty around the letter-box.

"Is my dinner hot?" asked the excessively late husband. "It should be," said his furious wife, "it's been on the fire since seven o'clock!"

I was a waiter at the Hotel
Splendiferous for three months,
but I had to leave on account of
the head waiter's nerves.
His nerves?
He couldn't stand the sound of
breaking crockery.

Did you hear about the ghoul's
favorite hotel?
It had running rot and mould in
every room.

John: Do you feel like a cup of tea?
Don: Oh, yes.
John: You look like one, too –
sloppy, hot and wet!

What's green and served hot from
the oven?
An idiot's salad.

There were two eggs boiling in a saucepan. One said "Phew, it's hot in here," the other said, "Wait till you get out, you'll get your head bashed in."

Hotel porter: May I carry your bag, sir?
Hotel guest: That won't be necessary, my wife is perfectly capable of walking.

How do you stop someone who's been working out in the gym on a hot day from smelling?
Put a peg on his nose!

What's the hottest letter of the alphabet?
"B." It makes oil boil.

Did you hear about the two men who
were cremated at the same time?
It was a dead heat.

What's the difference between
Father Christmas and a warm
dog?
Father Christmas wears a whole
suit, a dog just pants.

What do you get if you cross an elephant with some locusts?
I'm not sure, but if they ever swarm – watch out!

How do mice celebrate when they move house?
With a mouse-warming party.

What did the drone say to the Queen Bee?
"Swarm in here isn't it?"

Why does a witch wear a pointed black hat?
To keep her head warm.

Teacher: What do you think astronauts wear to keep warm?
Girl: Apollo neck jumpers?

Bill: This loaf is nice and warm!
Tim: It should be – the cat's been sitting on it all day!

Eddie was telling Freddie of his plans to make a lot of money. "I intend to buy a dozen swarms of bees and every morning at dawn I'm going to let them into the park opposite my house to spend all the day making honey, while I relax." "But the park doesn't open until nine o'clock," protested Freddie. "I realize that," said Eddie, "but I know where there's a hole in the fence."

Darren was showing Sharon his holiday photos. She admired all the scenery and the people. Then Darren showed her a picture of him having a donkey ride on the beach. "Who's that on your back?" asked Sharon.

What was proved when the fat man was run over by a steamroller? That he had a lot of guts.

Why did the farmer plow his field
with a steamroller?
Because he planned to grow
mashed potatoes.

"Your son is horribly spoiled," a
woman said to a proud mother one
day.
"How dare you!" retorted the
second woman. "My son's a
perfect little gentleman."
"I'm afraid you haven't seen what
the steamroller's done to him!"

What's the difference between
Frankenstein and boiled potatoes?
You can't mash Frankenstein.

1st cannibal: Come and have
dinner in our hut tonight.
2nd cannibal: What are you
having?
1st cannibal: Hard-boiled legs.

Wife, to husband: Boil the baby while I feed the potatoes, will you?

Psychiatrist: Well, what's your problem?

Patient: I prefer brown shoes to black shoes.

Psychiatrist: There's nothing wrong with that. Lots of people prefer brown shoes to black shoes. I do myself.

Patient: Really? How do your like yours – fried or boiled?

What do you call an English teacher,
five feet tall, covered from head to
toe in boils and totally bald?
Sir!

Heather: Help! I'm boiling!
Hyacinth: Oh, simmer down.

Giles: Can you lend me 10 cents? I
want to phone a friend.
Miles: Here's 25 cents. Phone all
your friends.

Summer Sensations

Where does an elephant go on holiday?
Tuscany.

What do you call a mosquito on holiday?
An itch-hiker.

What do you say to a hitch-hiking frog?
"Hop in!"

What do you get if you cross a frog
with a ferry?
A hoppercraft.

How do toads travel?
By hoppercraft.

Which Cornish town is the favorite
holiday spot for rodents?
Mousehole.

What do bees do if they want to
use public transport?
Wait at a buzz stop.

What happened when the cannibal
crossed the Atlantic on the QE2?
He told the waiter to take the
menu away and bring him the
passenger list.

Where do witches go for their
holidays?
Bat-lins.

Where did vampires go to first in
America?
New-fang-land.

Where do Chinese vampires come
from?
Fanghai.

Where do zombies go for cruises?
The Deaditerranean.

What do demons have on holiday?
A devil of a time.

Where do ghosts go on holiday?
The Ghosta Brava.

Where do ghost trains stop?
At devil crossings.

Why are ghosts at their loudest in
August?
Because they're on their
howlidays.

Which airway do ghouls fly with?
British Scareways.

Where do ghosts like to go on holiday?
Goole.

How did the rabbit get to Australia?
He flew by hareplane.

James: Do you know what nice people do on holiday?
John: No.
James: I didn't think you would.

Why couldn't the skeleton pay his
bus fare?
Because he was skint.

Why did the bat miss the bus?
Because he hung around too long.

Why do you have to wait so long for
a ghost train to come along?
They only run a skeleton service.

1st ghost: I died at Waterloo, you know.
2nd ghost: Really? Which platform.

1st witch: I'm going to France tomorrow.
2nd witch: Are you going by broom?
1st witch: No, by hoovercraft.

Did you hear about the ghost who
learned to fly?
He was pleased to be back on
terror-firma.

Where do ants go for their
holidays?
Fr-ants.

How do fleas travel?
Itch-hiking.

What steps should you take if you
see a dangerous yeti on your
travels?
Very large ones.

What do Paddington Bear and
Winnie the Pooh pack for their
holidays?
The bear essentials.

The seaside resort we went to last year was so boring that one day the tide went out and never came back.

My girlfriend talks so much that when she goes on holiday, she has to spread suntan lotion on her tongue.

Boss: You're looking much better now, Reynolds. How's that pain? Reynolds: She's away on a business trip.

Charlie was very nervous about going in a plane. "Do these planes crash often?" he asked the flight attendant. "No," she smiled, "only once."

Nellie: Our form mistress went to the West Indies for her holidays.
Kelly: Jamaica?
Nellie: No, she went of her own accord.

What can you see from the top of the Eiffel Tower?
Quite an eyeful!

Which American city would a cow
like to visit?
Moo York.

Crossing the Atlantic in a Rowing
Boat – by Eva Lott

Summertime – by Theresa Greene

Sarah: I'm going to sunbathe on my holiday. I love the sun.

Susie: Oh, so do I. I could lie in the sun all day and all night.

Darren went on a camping holiday with his family. "Did the tent leak?" asked his friend Sharon. "Only when it rained," answered Darren.

What did the sea say to the beach?
Nothing, it just waved.

Why did the principal like to take
her main holiday in the spring?
She liked clean sheets on her bed.

Lizzie got a bad case of sunburn.
When she complained how sore it
was, her brother remarked, "Well, I
guess you basked for it."

Passenger: Does this bus go to London?
Bus driver: No.
Passenger: But it says London on the front.
Bus driver: It says fish fingers on the side but we don't sell them!

In the summer holidays the math teacher collected information for a national opinion poll. But after a week she was sacked. Her vital statistics were wrong.

Mrs Broadbeam: Now, remember, children, travel is very good for you. It broadens the mind.

Sarah, muttering: If you're anything to go by, that's not all it broadens!

Pattie: We had a burglary last night, and they took everything except the soap and towels.

Peter: The dirty crooks.

A pilot flying over the jungle was having trouble with his plane and decided to bail out before it crashed. So he got into his parachute, jumped, pulled the rip-cord, and drifted gently down to land. Unfortunately he landed right in a large cooking pot which a tribal chief was simmering gently over a fire. The chief looked at him, rubbed his eyes, looked again, and asked, "What's this flier doing in my soup?"

After years of traveling around the world in his search, the wicked Abanazar finally discovered the enchanted cave in which he believed lay the magic lamp which would make him millions. He stood before the boulders which sealed the cave, and uttered the magic words, "Open, sesame!" There was a silence, and then a ghastly voice from within moaned, "Open says-a-who?"

Why did the stupid pilot land his plane on a house?
Because the landing lights were on.

What makes the Tower of Pisa lean?
It doesn't eat much.

Harry was telling his friend about his holiday in Switzerland. His friend had never been to Switzerland, and asked, "What did you think of the scenery?" "Oh, I couldn't see much," Harry admitted. "There were all those mountains in the way."

What's green, has four legs and two trunks?
Two seasick tourists.

"Why did you come back early from your holidays?" one of Alec's friends asked him. "Well, on the first day we were there one of the chickens died and that night we had chicken soup. The next day one of the pigs died and we had pork chops . . ." "But why did you come back?" "Well, on the third day the farmer's father-in-law died. What would you have done?"

A woman just back from the United States was telling her friends about the trip. "When my husband first saw the Grand Canyon, his face dropped a mile," she said. "Why, was he disappointed with the view?" "No, he fell over the edge."

What is the best thing to take into the desert?
A thirst-aid kit.

A new porter at a Paris hotel was instructed by the manager that it was important to call the guests by their names, in order to make them feel welcome and that the easiest way to find out their name was to look at their luggage. Armed with this advice, the porter took two guests up to their rooms, put down their bags and said, "I hope you 'ave a very 'appy stay 'ere in Paris, Mr and Mrs Genuine Cow'ide."

What do you think of this suit? I
had it made in Hong Kong.
Very nice, but what's that hump on
the back?
Oh, that's the tailor. He's still
working on it.

"I hope this plane doesn't travel
faster than sound," said the old
lady to the a flight attendant.
"Why?" "Because my friend and I
want to talk, that's why."

Last time my wife and I traveled on the ferry from Newhaven to Dieppe, we had six meals.
Six meals for that short crossing?
Three down and three up.

A naughty child was irritating all the passengers on the flight from London to New York. At last one man could stand it no longer. "Hey kid," he shouted, "Why don't you go outside and play?"

The transatlantic liner was experiencing particularly heavy weather, and Mrs Ramsbottom wasn't feeling well. "Would you care for some more supper, madam?" asked the steward. "No thanks," replied the wretched passenger. "Just throw it overboard to save me the trouble."

First explorer: There's one thing about Jenkinson.
Second explorer: What's that?
First explorer: He could go to headhunters' country without any fear – they'd have no interest in him.

Why is it not safe to sleep on trains?
Because they run over sleepers.

What is red outside, green and
hairy inside, and very crowded?
A bus full of gooseberries.

What's green and hairy and wears
sunglasses?
A gooseberry on holiday.

What's sweet, sour, dangerous and
travels?
Takeaway Kung food.

Where's a shark's favorite holiday
destination?
Finland.

How do nits go on holidays?
British Hairways.

Why won't midfield players travel
by airplane?
In case they are put on the wing.

What's red and wobbles on top of sponge cake and custard in the middle of Paris?
The Trifle Tower.

Kylie and Riley were talking about their forthcoming summer holidays. "Last year," said Kylie, "my brother and I took turns to bury each other in the sand." "Yes, but what about this year?" interrupted Riley. "I was coming to that," said Kylie. "This year we're going back to try to find him."

Local: Are you lost?
Stranger: No, I'm here. It's the bus station that's lost.

Letter from a travel agent: The flight you requested is fully booked but if someone falls out we'll let you know.

Notice at a railroad station: These toilets are out of order. Please use platform 6.

Louise: Did you hear about the stupid hitch-hiker?
Liza: No, what did he do?
Louise: He started his journey early so there wouldn't be so much traffic about.

Older brother: When I was a sailor I sailed both ways across the Atlantic without taking a bath.
Younger brother: I always said you were a dirty double crosser!

My Uncle Ben and Aunt Flo
haven't had a row for five years.
That's wonderful.
Not really. Uncle Ben lives in
China.

What happens when a plane runs
out of fuel?
All the passengers get out to push.

Super Slanders

What happens if you eat too much candy?
You take up two seats on the bus!

The school had given a concert and Mrs Feather's son had played the piano. She was very proud of him. She asked his music teacher, "Do you think my Freddie should take up the piano as a career?"
"No," replied the music teacher, "I think he should put down the lid as a favor."

Ben's sister, Samantha, wanted to be an actress when she left school. "Is she pretty?" asked Bill. "Let's just say she has a perfect face for radio," answered Ben.

Nellie: I have an open mind.
Kelly: Yes, there's nothing in it.

Brian: How long can someone live without a brain?
Ryan: How old are you?

Lyn: I don't like soup.
Brian: I expect you can't get it to stay on the fork.

Trixie: When I die I'm going to leave my brain to science.
Tracey: I suppose every little helps.

Mick: Tim's gone to live in the city.
Nick: Why's that?
Mick: He'd read in the papers that the country was at war.

Man in clothes store: I'd like a blue shirt to match my eyes, please.
Sales clerk: I'm sorry, sir, we don't have any blue shirts. But we do have some soft hats that would match your head.

Did you hear about the boy who
was known as Fog?
He was thick and wet.

Jen: You look as if you'd find it
hard to chew gum and walk at the
same time.
Ken: And you look as if you'd find
it hard to chew gum and breathe
at the same time!

Barry: You're like uncultivated woodland.
Gary: Really?
Barry: Yes, totally dense.

Jane: Do you ever do any gardening?
Wayne: Not often. Why?
Jane: You look as if you could do with some remedial weeding.

Holly: Do you ever find life boring?
Dolly: I didn't until I met you.

He's so stupid he thinks a
cucumber is something you play
snooker with.

She's so stupid she thinks
Christmas Eve is a tug of war.

Charlie: Do you think I'm intelligent?
Chrissie: I'd like to say "yes" but my Mom says I must always tell the truth.

Emma: I'd like to say something nice about you as it's your birthday.
Gemma: Why don't you?
Emma: Because I can't think of a single thing to say!

Ivan: They say Ian has a dual personality.
Ivor: Let's hope the other one is brighter than this one!

Madge: Your body's quite well organized.
Martin: How do you mean?
Madge: The weakest part – your brain – is protected by the strongest – your thick skull!

Suresh: Whatever will Clive do when he leaves school? I can't see him being bright enough to get a job.

Sandra: He could always be a ventriloquist's dummy.

Hazel: I wonder what my IQ is?

Heather: Don't worry about it, it's nothing.

I always like to think the best of people, that's why I think of you as a complete idiot.

"She has a mind of her own." "Of course she does. No one else would want it."

Did you hear someone has invented a coffin that just covers the head? It's for people like you who're dead from the neck up!

Bertie: You remind me of a Greek statue.
Gertie: Do you mean you think I'm beautiful?
Bertie: Yes, beautiful, but not all there.

Roy: They say ignorance is bliss.
Rita: Then you should be the happiest boy in the world.

Bennie: I've been told I must lose
5 kg of surplus fat.
Kenny: You could always cut off
your head.

Cary: There's no point in telling you
a joke with a double meaning.
Mary: Why not?
Cary: You wouldn't get either of
them.

I'd like you to accept my opinion for what it's worth.
That means you owe me one cent.

My brother said he'd tell me everything he knows.
He must have been speechless.

Stella: Tracey has a ready wit.
Sheila: Perhaps she could let us know when it's ready!

Daniel: Being clever isn't
everything.
Denzil: In your case it isn't
anything.

My sister's going out with David.
Any girl who goes out with David
must be able to appreciate the
simpler things in life.

They say Margaret is a raving beauty.
You mean she's escaped from a loony bin?

In one way Julian is lucky. If he went out of his mind no one would notice the difference.

I feel sorry for your little mind – all alone in that great big head.

Jonathan ought to be a boxer.
Someone might knock him
conscious.

Why is your brother always flying
off the handle?
Because he's got a screw loose.

Marie: Two heads are better than
one.
Gary: In your case none might be
better than one!

His speech started at 2 p.m. sharp.
And finished at 3 p.m. dull.

They call him Baby-face.
Does that mean he has a brain to
match?

Brian: Let's play a game of wits.
Diane: No, Let's play something
you can play too.

They say many doctors have examined her brain – but they can't find anything in it.

Don't let your mind wander. It's not strong enough to be allowed out on its own.

Jane: Do you like me?
Wayne: As girls go, you're fine.
And the sooner you go the better!

Handsome Harry: Every time I walk past a girl she sighs.
Wisecracking William: With relief!

Freda: Boys whisper they love me.
Fred: Well, they wouldn't admit it out loud, would they?

Jerry: Is that a new perfume I smell?
Kerry: It is, and you do!

Laura: Whenever I go to my local shop the shopkeeper shakes my hand.
Lionel: I expect it's to make sure you don't put it in his till.

Bernie: Why have you given me this piece of rope?
Ernie: They say if you give someone enough rope they'll hang themselves!

Peter: My brother wants to work badly.

Anita: As I remember, he usually does.

Michael: It's hard for my sister to eat.

Maureen: Why?

Michael: She can't bear to stop talking.

Boss: Are you willing to do an honest day's work?
Secretary: Yes, as long as you give me an honest week's pay for it.

Son: How old are you, Dad?
Dad: Oh, around 35.
Son: I expect you've been around it a few times!

My brother's looking for a wife.
Trouble is, he can't find a woman
who loves him as much as he loves
himself.

He reminds me of a bowl of custard.
Yes, yellow and thick.

They say he works eight hours and
sleeps eight hours.
Problem is, they're the same eight
hours.

My dad once stopped a man ill-
treating a donkey.
It was a case of brotherly love.

Gordon: My wallet's full of big
bills.
Graham: All unpaid, I expect.

Jimmy: Is that lemonade OK?
Timmy: Yes. Why do you ask?
Jimmy: I just wondered if it was as
sour as your face.

Lee: Our family's descended from royalty.
Dee: King Kong?

Anne: Do you think I look awful in this dress?
Dan: You could look worse – if I had better eyesight!

Mary: Do you think my sister's pretty?
Gary: Well, Let's just say if you pulled her pigtail she'd probably say "oink, oink."

Cheryl: They say I have an infectious laugh.
Meryl: In that case don't laugh near me!

"Do you like my new baby sister?
The stork brought her." "Hmm, it
looks as if the stork dropped her
on her head."

My sister went on a crash diet.
Is that why she looks a wreck?

My brother's on a seafood diet.
Really?
Yes, the more he sees food the
more he eats.

Penny: No one could call your dad a quitter.
Kenny: No, he's been sacked from every job he's ever had.

Winnie: I was cut out to be a genius.
Ginny: Pity no one put the pieces together properly.

Terry: When my mother was young she had a coming-out party.
Gerry: When they saw her they probably sent her back in again.

I hear she was a war baby.
I'm not surprised – I expect her parents took one look at her and started fighting.

Does he have a big mouth?
Put it this way, he can sing a duet
by himself.

Does your brother keep himself
clean?
Oh, yes. He takes a bath every
month whether he needs one or
not.

His left eye must be fascinating.
Why do you say that?
Because his right eye looks at it all
the time.

How can she be so fat? She eats
like a bird!
Yes, a vulture!

She once had a million-dollar
figure.
Trouble is, inflation set in.

My boyfriend only has two faults –
everything he says and everything
he does!

I hear he's a very careful person.
Well, he likes to economize on soap
and water.

That girl looks like Helen Black.
She looks even worse in white.

Rich Lady: That painting you did of me doesn't do me justice.
Artist: It's not justice you want, it's mercy!

New Wife: Will you love me when I'm old and fat and ugly?
New Husband: Of course I do!

She's so ugly that when a wasp stings her it shuts its eyes.

Bill and Gill make a perfect pair,
don't they?
They certainly do. She's a pill and
he's a headache

They say she has a sharp tongue.
Yes, she can slice bread with it.

They say cleanliness is next to
godliness.
With some people it's next to
impossible!

Does he tell lies?
Let's just say his memory
exaggerates.

Jane: I'll cook dinner. What would
you like?
Shane: Good life insurance.

Harry's very good for other people's
health.
Whenever they see him coming
they go for a long walk!

Did you say he had a big mouth?
Put it this way, he's the only person
I know who can eat a banana
sideways!

She could give a headache to an
aspirin!

He's watching his weight.
Yes, watching it go up!

He's a light eater.
Yes, as soon as it's light he starts
eating!

Does he have big ears?
Let's just say he's very good at
swatting flies.

Dickie: I hear the team's prospects
are looking up.
Nicky: Oh good, are you leaving it
then?

Bob had just missed a shot at goal, which meant the other team won. "I could kick myself," he groaned, as the players came off the pitch. "Don't bother," said the captain, "you'd miss."

The last time I saw a face like yours I threw it a banana.

Canteen Lady: Do you want more of this custard?
Boy: No thanks, I'm too young to die.

Boy: Have you got any custard left?
Canteen Lady: Yes.
Boy: Well you shouldn't have made so much then.

Customer: Two soggy eggs on burnt toast, please.

Café Owner: We can't serve that here, sir.
Customer: Why not, you did yesterday.

What happened when the umpire had a brain transplant?
The brain rejected him.

What did they call the crazy golfer?
A crack putt!

Golfer: Have you packed all my golf gear in the car?

Wife: Yes, dear: clubs, map, compass, emergency rations . . .

Despondent Golfer: I'd move heaven and earth to get a better score.

Caddie: Concentrate on heaven, you've already moved enough earth!

Gloria: Boys fall in love with me at first sight.
Gordon: Yes, but when they take a second look they change their mind!

Harold: We should all try to fight air pollution.
Henry: You could start by stopping breathing.

Comedian: Do you find me
entertaining?
Friend: I'd say you were too dumb
to entertain a thought.

Boss: It would take ten men to fill
my shoes.
Secretary, Aside: It looks as if it
took ten cows to make them.

Samantha: Don't I look gorgeous today?
Susannah: It's a treat for people to see you. After all, they have to pay to get into a freak show.

His clothes never go out of style – they look just as old-fashioned every year.

He's so stupid he probably couldn't spell "Anna" backwards.

"He can't see further than the nose on his face." "No, but with his nose that's quite a distance."

Diner: Will the band play requests?
Waiter: Yes, sir. What would you like?
Diner: I'd like them to play cards.

I'm as pretty as a flower.
Yes, a cauliflower.

He asked me to tell him everything
I know.
I bet you were speechless.

Words fail me.
I'd noticed you don't know how to
use them.

He thinks he's a big cheese.
I certainly have to hold my nose
when I'm near him.

He's such a whinger – if
opportunity knocked he'd complain
about the noise.

He's the kind of boy girls dream
about.
That's better than seeing him in
broad daylight.

You know how nurses slap babies
when they are born?
Yes.

Well, when you were born I reckon
they took one look and slapped
your mother.

What do you think of Ada's looks?
I don't mind her looking, it's her
face I can't stand.

Monty: Does a mud pack help her
complexion?
Bunty: It does for a few days, but
then the mud falls off.

They say when the photographer
took Jim's photograph he never
developed it.
Why?
He was afraid of being alone with
it in a dark room.

The problem is, his facial features
don't seem to understand the
importance of being part of a
team.

Do you think I have a good complexion?
Let's just say your face is almost as smooth as a walnut.

Rosie: I like being tickled under the chin.
Josie: Which one?

Nigel has a Roman nose.
Yes, it's roamin' here, roamin there . . ."

I think she's quite old, don't you?
She has so many wrinkles on her
forehead she has to screw on her
hat.

She's not very fat, is she?
No, she's got a really faminine
look.
Her sister's skinny, too.
Yes, if she drinks tomato juice she
looks like a thermometer.

Kylie: My uncle's just bought a pig.
Riley: But where will he keep it?
Kylie: Under the bed.
Riley: But what about the smell?
Kylie: The pig will just have to get used to it.

His death won't be listed under "Obituaries," it will be under "Neighborhood Improvements."

She's so ugly that even spiders run away when they see her.

Susie: I think a lot of people would go to our principal's funeral.
Sally: Yes, to make sure she's dead!

Kate: I always speak my mind.
Kath: I'm surprised you've so much
to say, then.

Jimmy: Go and squirt lemon juice
in your eyes.
Timmy: Whatever for?
Jimmy: It's the only way to make
you smart.

You remind me of a toenail.
What do you mean?
The sooner you're cut down to size
the better.

What's the difference between a
bully and gravy?
Gravy's only thick some of the
time.

Stella: You only have one use in life.
Ella: What's that?
Stella: Your face can cure hiccups!

Claud: What's the difference between you and a skunk?
Maud: I don't know.
Claud: You use a cheaper deodorant.

Darren: I'm so thirsty my tongue's
hanging out.
Sharon: Is that your tongue? I
thought it was a horrible spotted
tie!

Bernie: What's the matter with
your finger?
Ernie: I think I've got a splinter in it.
Bernie: Have you been scratching
your head?

Angus: Have you been talking to yourself again?
Adam: Yes, how did you know?
Angus: You've got that bored look on your face.

Glyn: You remind me of a builder's bottom.
Wyn: What do you mean?
Glyn: You're full of barefaced cheek!

Patty: What smells worse than a bad egg?
Mattie: I don't know.
Patty: You do!

What do you mean she eats like a bird? She's enormous!
I expect she eats worms.

Gilly: Do you like my cottage pie?
Billy: No, it tastes as if you've left the drains in it.

Diner: This food isn't fit for a pig!
Waiter: I'll bring you some that is, sir.

I never forget a face – but in your case I'll make an exception.

Mr Black: I took my wife to the beauty parlor yesterday and I had to sit and wait all afternoon for her.

Mr White: Whatever was she having done?

Mr Black: Nothing – she just went for an estimate.

Mrs Brown: I took my son to the zoo yesterday.

Mrs Green: Did they accept him?

Hear about the stupid builder? He put a notice saying "Stop" on the top of his ladder.

Louise: What's the difference between you and a baby lamb?
Lionel: I don't know.
Louise: The lamb will one day be a sheep, but you'll always be a creep.

Andy: My dad's stronger than your dad.

Mandy: He must be after raising a dumb-bell like you!

Lesley: Did she really call you a creep?

Wesley: Yes. She said I was lower than the fluff in an earthworm's belly button.

Cool Connections

Darren, who was rather fond of Sharon, gave her a box of chocolates at break time on her birthday. "Here you are," he said, blushing, "sweets to the sweet." "Oh, thanks," said Sharon. "Have a nut."

Hear about the woman who wanted to marry a ghost? I can't think what possessed her.

Why did Frankenstein's monster
squeeze his girlfriend to death?
He had a crush on her.

1st witch: I'm so unlucky.
2nd witch: Why?
1st witch: Last night I went to a
party and met a handsome prince.
2nd witch: What's unlucky about
that?
1st witch: When I kissed him he
turned into a frog.

I bet I could get you to forget about that horrible witch.
What horrible witch?
See, you've forgotten already.

First boy: She had a beautiful pair of eyes, her skin had the glow of a peach, her cheeks were like apples and her lips like cherries – that's my girl.
Second boy: Sounds like a fruit salad to me.

Two men were having a drink together. One said, "I'd rather live with a vampire than with my wife." "Why's that?" asked the other. He said, "Because she's always trying to bite my head off."

The man tried to poison his wife again. This time she lay on the floor shouting "Wretch, wretch, wretch!" He said, "No, you retch – you took the poison."

A lady put a lonely hearts ad in the paper and had a reply which said, "I would love to meet you but I have to tell you that I am eight feet tall, covered in matted fur, with large fangs and slobbering lips. If you still want to meet me then I'll be under the clock in the market square at six o'clock next Saturday." The lady replied, "I would be interested in meeting you but please will you wear a red carnation and carry a rolled-up newspaper so I can recognize you?"

Who is a vampire likely to fall in love with?
The girl necks door.

Me and the Wife – by Ian Shee.

Who was that I saw you with last night?
It was a girl from the school?
Teacher?
Didn't have to!

When Wally Witherspoon proposed
to his girlfriend she said, "I love
the simple things in life, Wally, but I
don't want one of them for a
husband."

A woman was in court charged
with wounding her husband. "But
madam, why did you stab him over
100 times?" asked the judge. "Oh,
your Honor," replied the
defendant, "I didn't know how to
switch off the electric carving
knife."

Two girls were talking in the corridor. "That boy over there is getting on my nerves," said Clarrie. "But he's not even looking at you," replied Clara. "That's what's getting on my nerves," retorted Clarrie.

What did the two acrobats say when they got married?
We're head over heels in love!

My girlfriend thinks I'm a great wit.
Well, she's half right.

A horrible old witch surprised all her friends by announcing that she was going to get married. "But," said another old hag, "you always said men were stupid. And you vowed never to marry." "Yes, I know," said the witch. "But I finally found one who asked me."

"The girl beside me in math is very clever," said Alec to his mother. "She's got enough brain for two."
"Perhaps you'd better think of marriage," said Mom.

I can't understand why people say my girlfriend's legs look like matchsticks.
They do look like sticks – but they certainly don't match.

Ben's new girlfriend uses such greasy lipstick that he has to sprinkle his face with sand to get a better grip.

"What's your new perfume called?" a young man asked his girlfriend. "High Heaven," she replied. "I asked what it was called, not what it smells to!"

"What do you do?" a young man asked the beautiful girl he was dancing with. "I'm a nurse." "I wish I could be ill and let you nurse me," he whispered in her ear. "That would be miraculous. I work on the maternity ward."

I'm suffering from bad breath. You should do something about it! I did. I just sent my wife to the dentist.

"What's the matter?" one man asked another. "My wife left me when I was in the bath last night," sobbed the second man. "She must have been waiting for years for the chance," replied the first.

Poor old Stephen sent his photograph off to a Lonely Hearts Club.
They sent it back saying that they weren't that lonely.

Freddie had persuaded Amanda to marry him, and was formally asking her father for his permission. "Sir," he said, "I would like to have your daughter for my wife." "Why can't she get one of her own?" replied Amanda's father.

Why aren't you married?
I was born that way.

Mrs Jones and her little daughter Karen were outside the church watching all the comings and goings of a wedding. After the photographs had been taken, everyone had driven off to the reception and all the excitement was over Karen said to her mother, "Why did the bride change her mind, Mommy?" How do you mean, change her mind?" asked Mrs Jones. "Well said the moppet, she went into the church with one man and came out with another."

Why did you refuse to marry
Richard, Tessa?
'Cos he said he would die if I
didn't and I'm just curious.

My Peter keeps telling everyone
he's going to marry the most
beautiful girl in the world.
What a shame! And after all the
time you've been engaged!

"But she's so young to get married," sobbed Diana's mother. "Only seventeen!" "Try not to cry about it," said her husband soothingly. "Think of it not as losing a daughter but as gaining a bathroom."

"Doctor Sawbones speaking." "Oh, doctor, my wife's just dislocated her jaw. Can you come over in, say, three or four weeks' time?"

A salesman was trying to persuade a housewife to buy a life insurance policy. "Just imagine, if your husband were to die," he said. "What would you get?" "Oh a sheepdog, I think," replied the wife. "They're so well-behaved."

My wife says that if I don't give up golf she'll leave me.
Say, that's tough, old man.
Yeah, I'm going to miss her.

Mrs Brown was always complaining about her husband. "If things go on like this I'll have to leave him," she moaned to Mrs Jenkins. "Give him the soft-soap treatment," said Mrs Jenkins. "I tried that," replied Mrs Brown, "it didn't work. He spotted it at the top of the stairs."

Mommy, mommy, why do you keep poking daddy in the ribs? If I don't, the fire will go out.

My husband really embarrassed me yesterday. We were at the vicarage for tea and he drank his with his little finger sticking out. But that's considered polite in some circles.
Not with the teabag hanging from it, it's not.

Mr Brown: I hate to tell you, but your wife just fell in the wishing well.
Mr Smith: It works!

Wife to husband: I'll have you know
I've got the face of a teenager!
Husband to wife: Then you should
give it back, you're wearing it out.

Bill: What would it take to make
you give me a kiss?
Gill: An anesthetic.

Harry: I've a soft spot for you.
Mary: Really?
Harry: Yes, in the middle of a bog!

James: I call my girlfriend Peach.
John: Because she's beautiful?
James: No, because she's got a
heart of stone!

Romeo: I'd go to the end of the earth for you.
Juliet: Good. And when you get there, jump off!

Judge: Your first three wives died from eating poisonous mushrooms, and now your fourth wife has drowned in your swimming-pool. Isn't that all a bit odd?
Prisoner: Not really. She didn't like mushrooms.

They say he has a leaning towards blondes.
Yes, but they keep pushing him back.

My boyfriend only has two faults –
everything he says and everything
he does!

I hear she doesn't care for a man's
company.
Not unless he owns it.

My sister fell in love at second
sight.
When she first met him she didn't
know how rich he was.

I got a gold watch for my
girlfriend.
I wish I could make a trade like
that!

What do you call pigs who live
together?
Pen pals.

What's the best way to get rid of
excess fat?
Divorce him.

When my mom and dad got engaged she asked him if he would be giving her a ring. Her said, "Of course. What's your number?"

What will you do when you're as big as your dad?
Go on a diet!

Eskimo girl: There's something I'd like to give you.

Eskimo boy: What?
Eskimo girl: The cold shoulder.

Wife: Did you like the food I
cooked for you?
Husband: Let's just say it was a
real swill dinner.

Barney: My girlfriend's cooking's like a good man.
Arnie: What do you mean?
Barney: Hard to keep down!

Wife: Did you really marry me because you'd heard my uncle had left me a fortune?
Husband: No, I'd have married you no matter who had left you a fortune.

My wife is very dear to me.
Yes, I believe she costs you a
fortune.

My husband's a millionaire.
He was a multi-millionaire before
you married him.

My girlfriend loves nature.
That's very good of her,
considering what nature has done
for her!

How are you getting on with
James?

Well, he's a bit dull until you get to
know him.

And when you have got to know
him you'll find he's a real bore!

He is pretty boring.

Yes, but he does have occasional
moments of silence.

Husband: You took me for better or worse.

Wife: Yes, but I didn't think it would be this much worse.

Wife: We've been married 12 whole months.

Husband: Seems more like a year to me.

Wife: One more word from you and I'm going back to mother!
Husband: Taxi!

They say he's her idol.
He certainly never does anything.

Myron: I can marry anyone I please!
Byron: But you don't please anyone!

Saul: My wife worships me.
Paul: Why do you think that?
Saul: She puts burnt offerings in front of me three times a day.

Wife: I've given you the best years of my life.
Husband: Are you asking me for a receipt?

Foreign visitor: And is this your most charming wife?
Husband: No, she's the only one I've got.

She talks so much he's never on speaking terms with her, just listening terms!

Can your husband cook?
Let's just say that yesterday he burned the salad.

Why do you call your girlfriend
Treasure?
Because I wonder where she was
dug up!

Kerry: My girlfriend's different
from all other girls.
Terry: I bet she's different. She's
the only girl around who'll go out
with you!

When he told me he loved me he said he'd go through anything for me.
And has he?
So far he's only gone through my bank account.

Billy: Since I met you I haven't been able to eat or drink.
Tilly: Because you love me so much?
Billy: No, because I'm broke.

Young man: I've come to ask for your daughter's hand.
Father: You'll have to take the rest of her too or the deal's off.

Why do they call her an after-dinner speaker?
Because every time she speaks to a man she's after a dinner.

William: Bob's so suspicious, isn't he?

Wilfred: Yes. Even his eyes watch each other all the time.

Stan: You remind me of the sea.

Sue: Because I'm so wild and romantic?

Stan: No, because you make me sick!

Jack: I was chosen by a computer as being an ideal boyfriend.
John: A computer's about the only thing that would have you as a boyfriend.

If we get married do you think you'll be able to live on my income? Of course. But what will you live on?

Tom: Could you be happy with a boy like me?

Trish: Maybe, if you weren't around too often.

Mrs Rose: Where are you going to?
Mrs Thorn: The doctor's. I don't like the look of my husband.
Mrs Rose: Can I come with you? I can't stand the sight of mine!

Holly: How are you getting on with your advertisements for a husband? Have you had any replies?
Molly: Yes, lots. And they all say the same – take mine!

Clark: I'm not rich like Arwin, and I don't have a country estate like Brian or a Ferrari like Clive, but I love you and I want to marry you.

Clara: I love you too, but what did you say about Brian?

Brian: Why are you covered with scratches?

Byron: My girlfriend said it with flowers.

Brian: That sounds romantic.

Byron: It wasn't, she hit me round the head with a bunch of roses.

Samantha: Do you really love me?
Simon: Oh yes.
Samantha: Then whisper
something soft and sweet in my
ear.
Simon: Lemon meringue pie.

Wife: Today we're having Chicken
Surprise.
Husband: What's the surprise?
Wife: You're cooking it.

Bridegroom: Will you really be able to put up with me for the rest of your life?

Bride: Of course, dear, you'll be out at work most of the time!

First man: Is your wife fat?

Second man: Put it this way, when we were married and I carried her across the threshold I had to make two trips.

Romeo: Will you come to the movies with me tonight?
Juliet: Oh, no, I never go out with perfect strangers.
Romeo: Who says I'm perfect?

Juliet: Whisper those three little words that will make my day.
Romeo: Go to hell!

They say she's been asked to get
married hundreds of times.
Really? Who by?
Her parents!